Vehicles, Planes and Trucks Coloring Book for kids and toddlers - activity books for preschooler - coloring book for Boys, Girls, for kids ages 2-4, 4-8)

This notebook belongs to

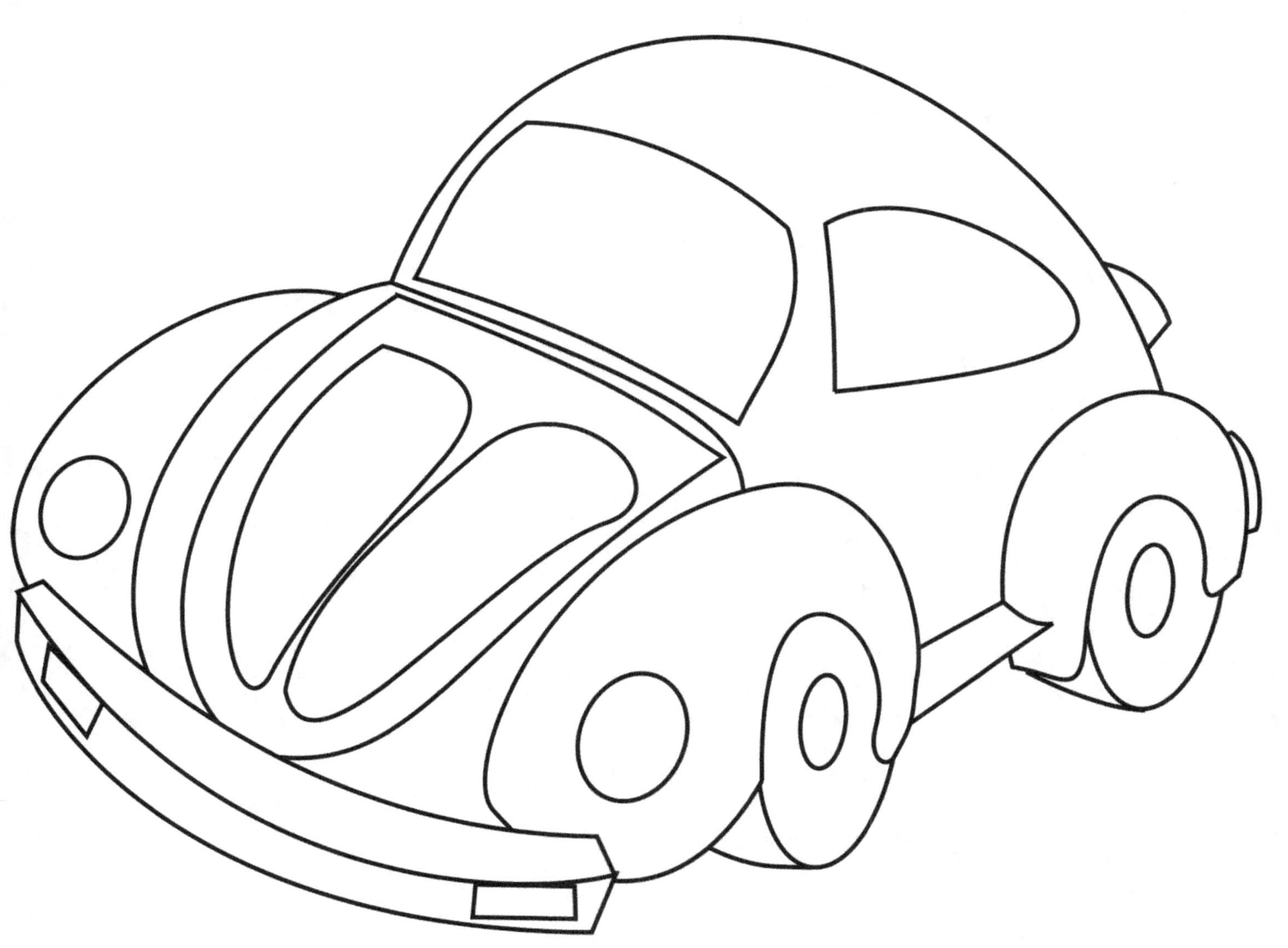

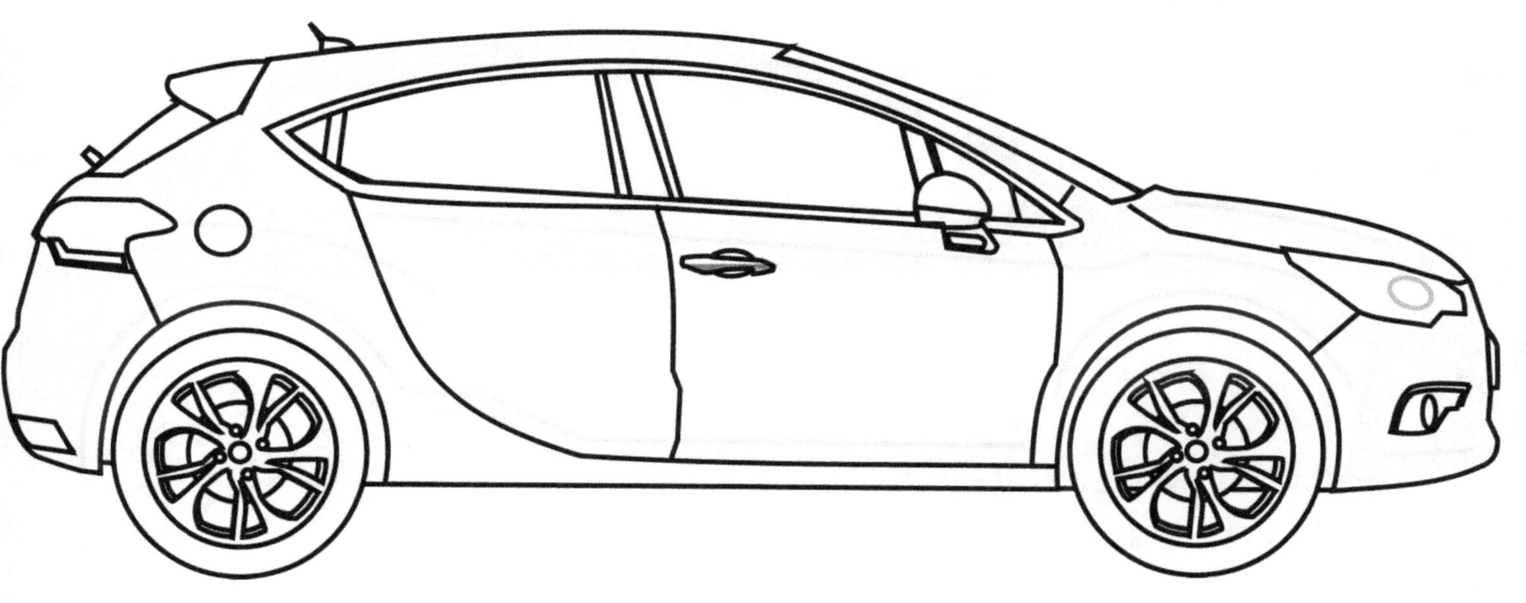

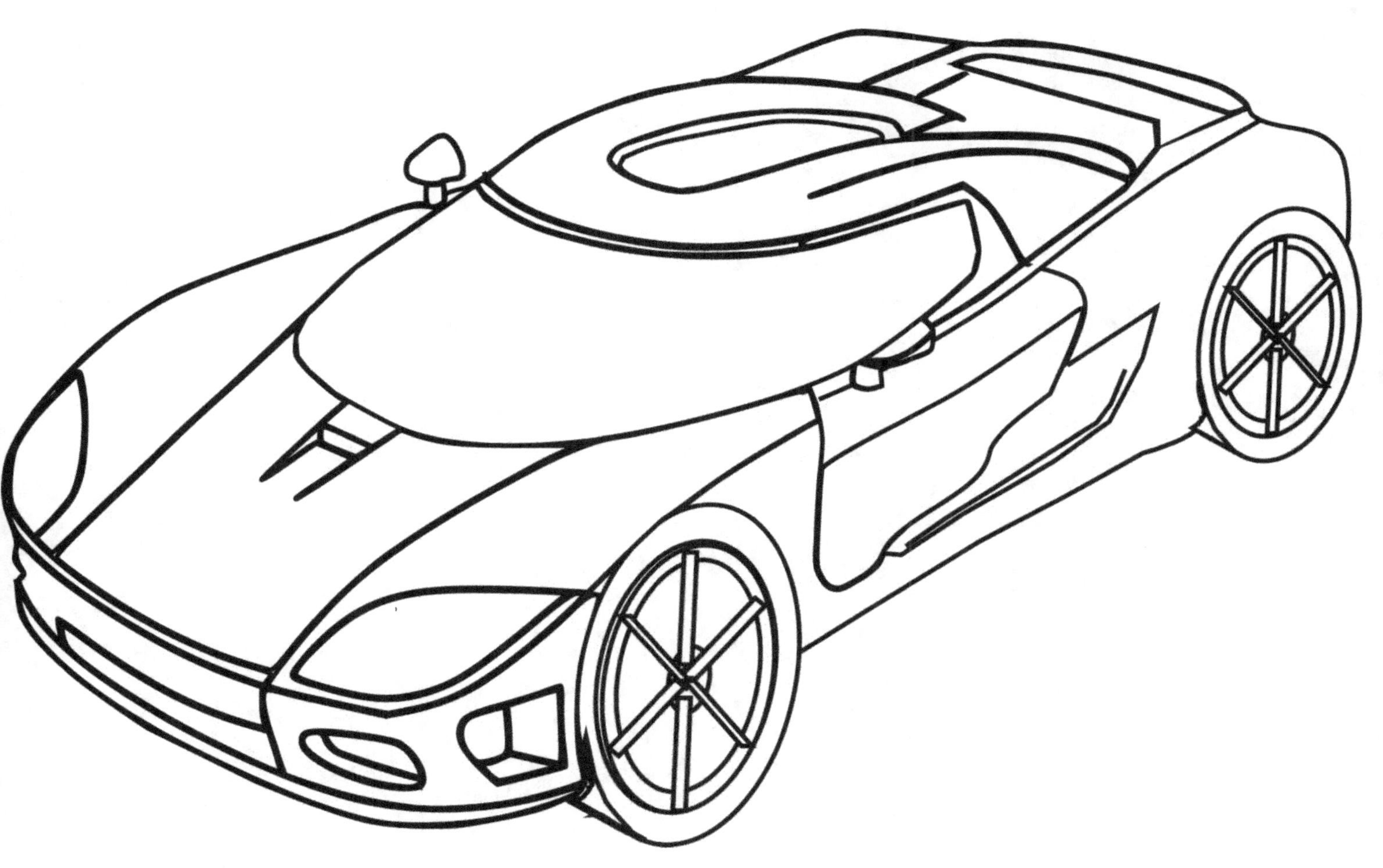

TOY

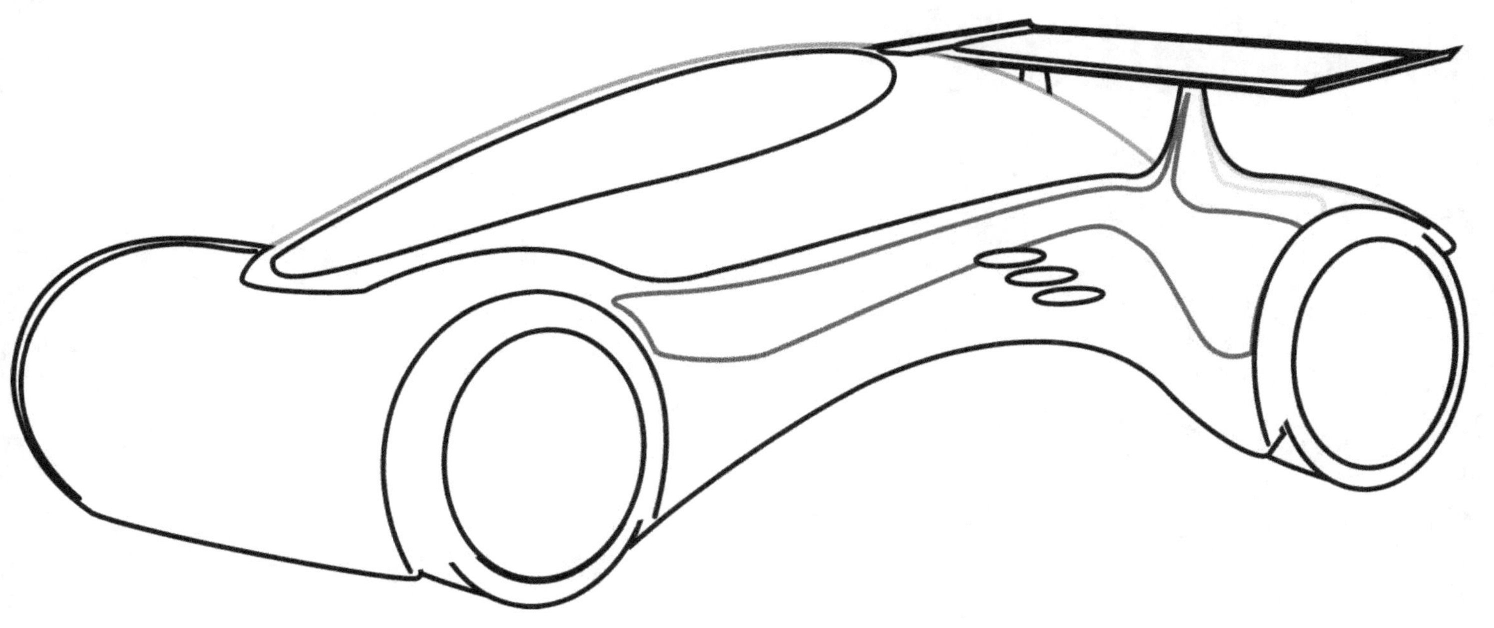

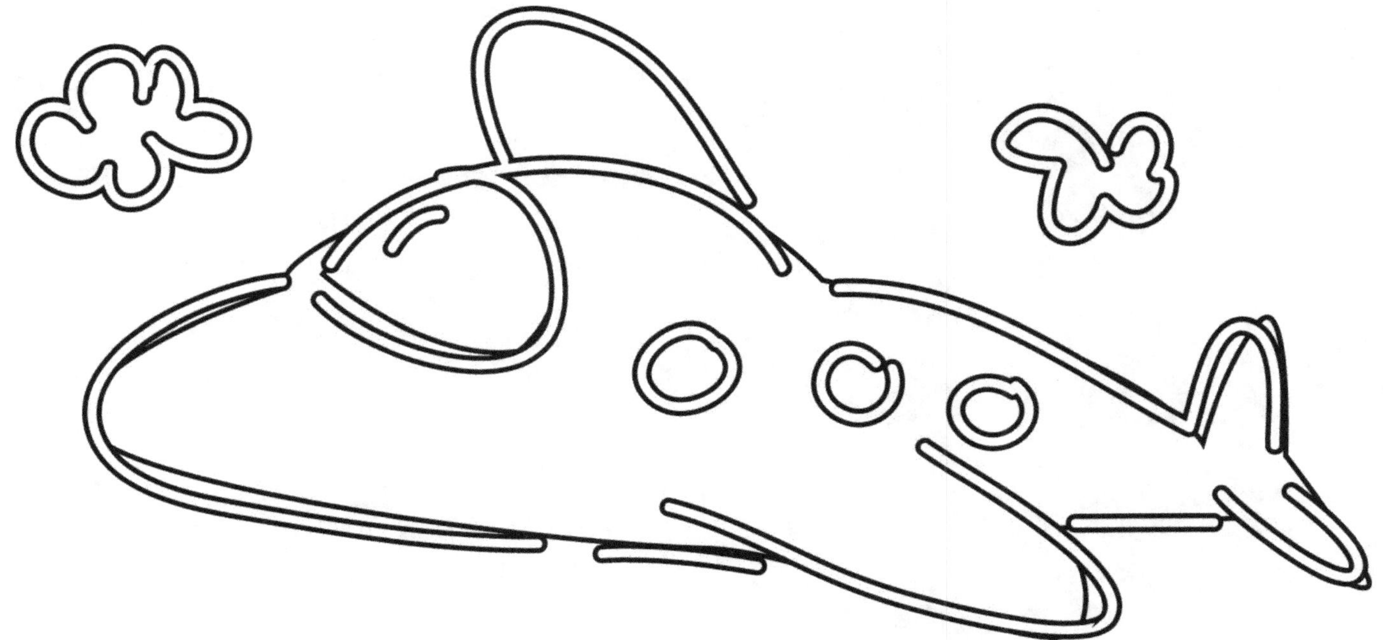

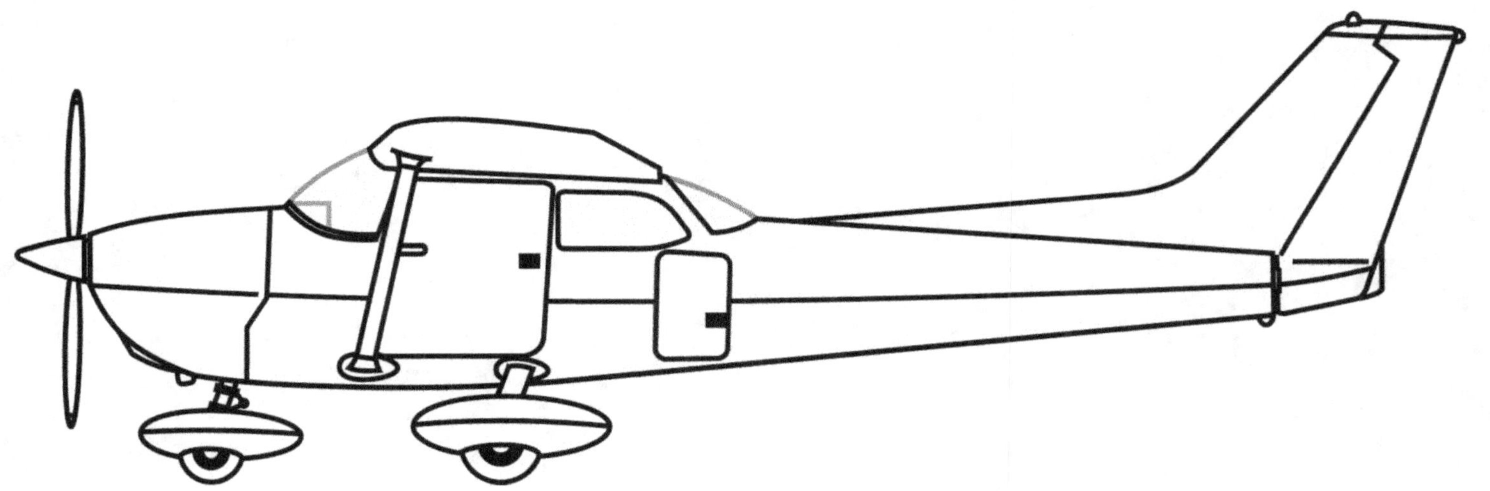

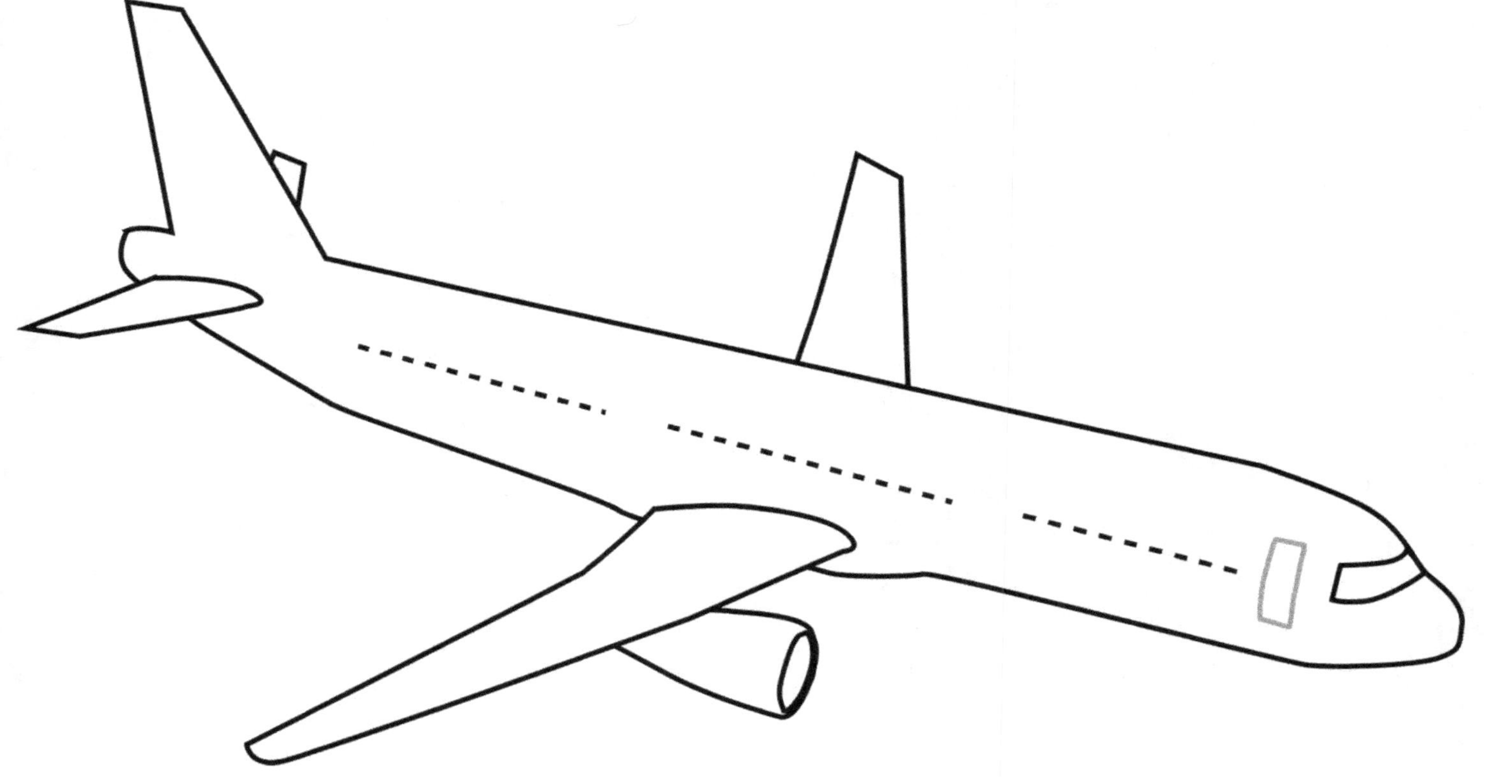

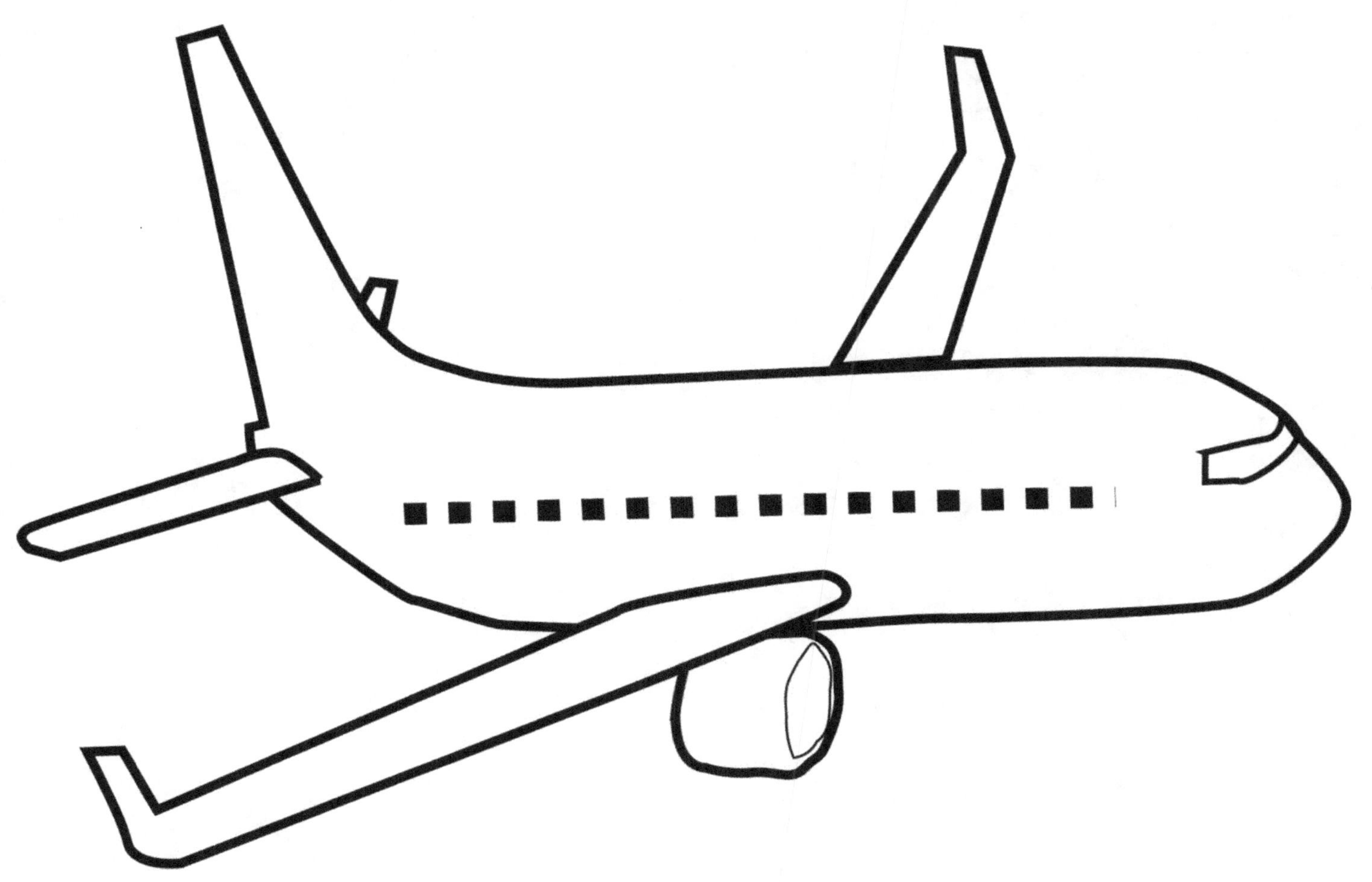

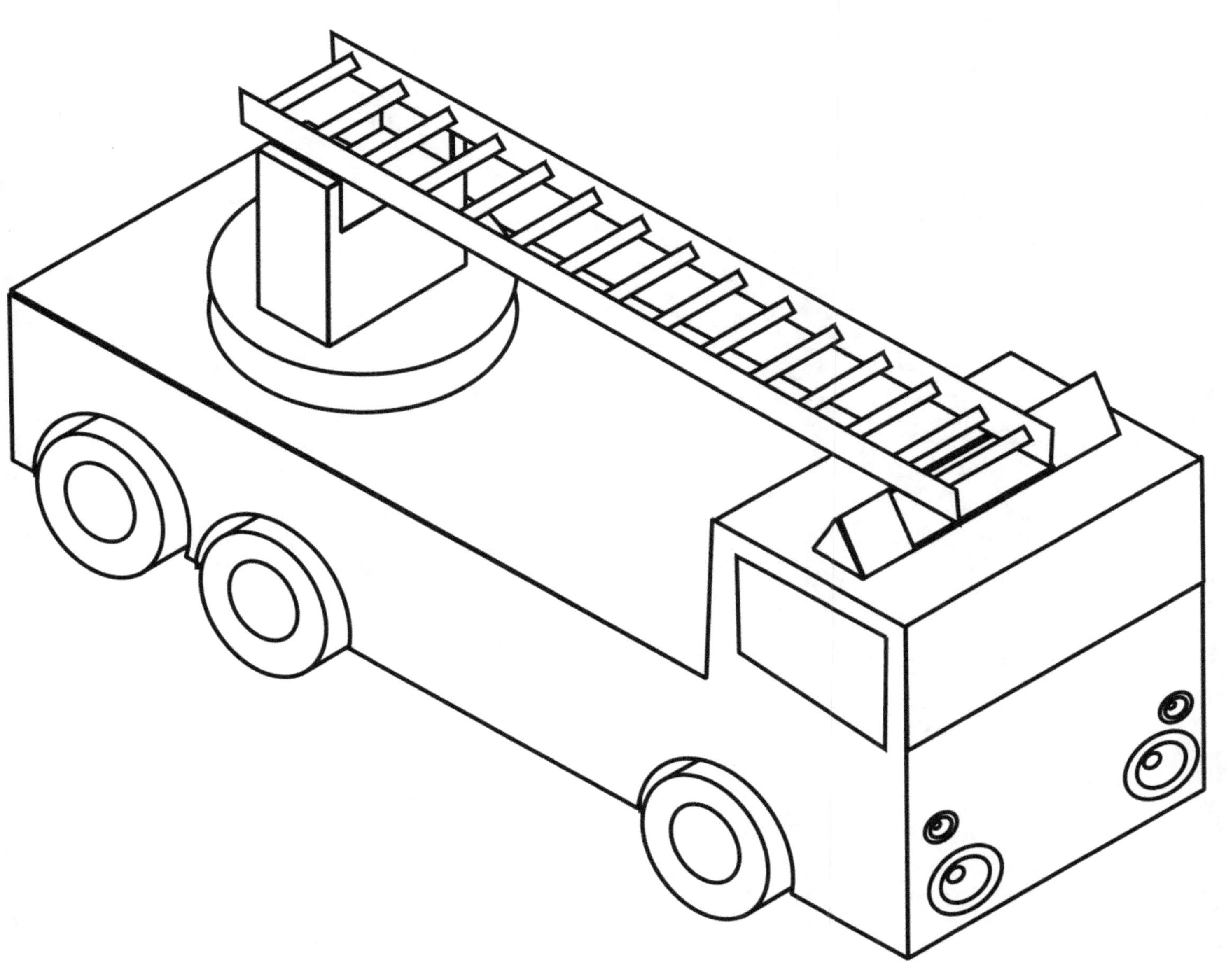

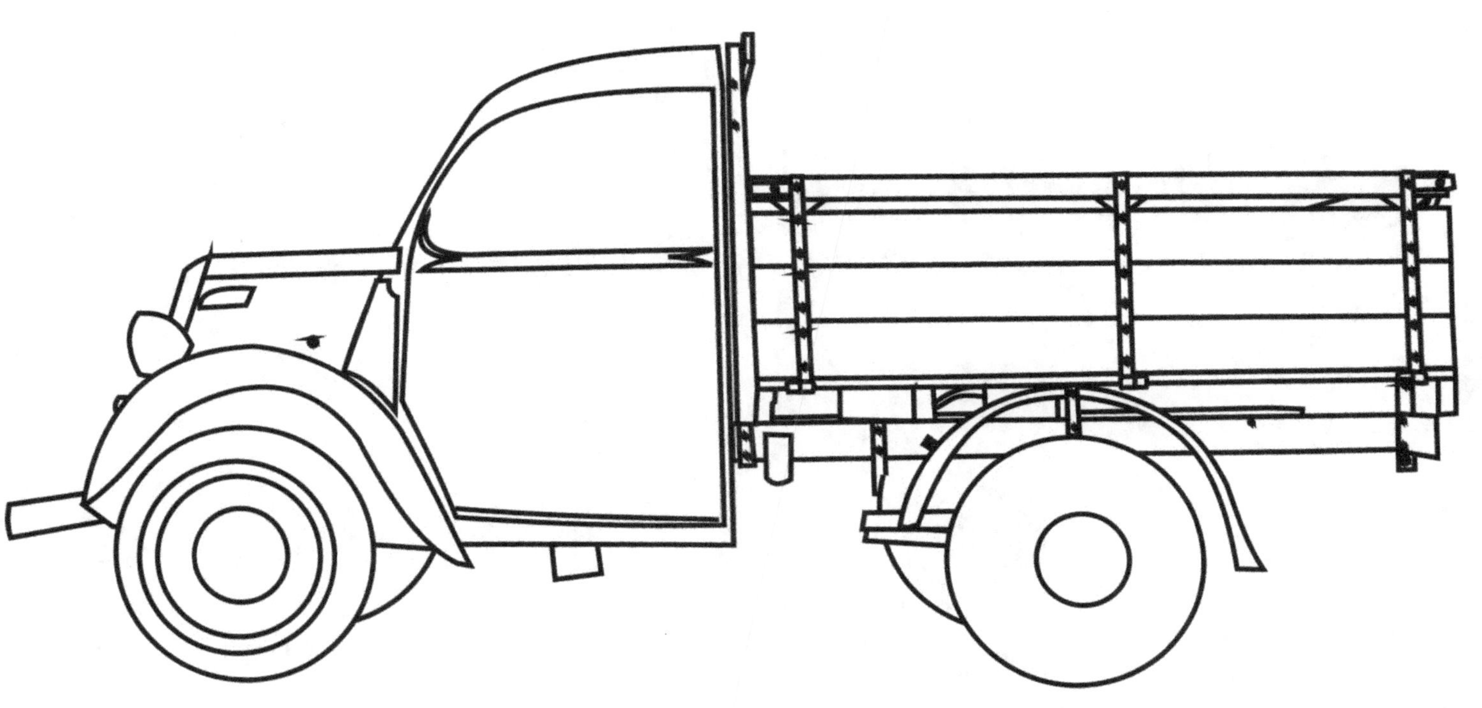

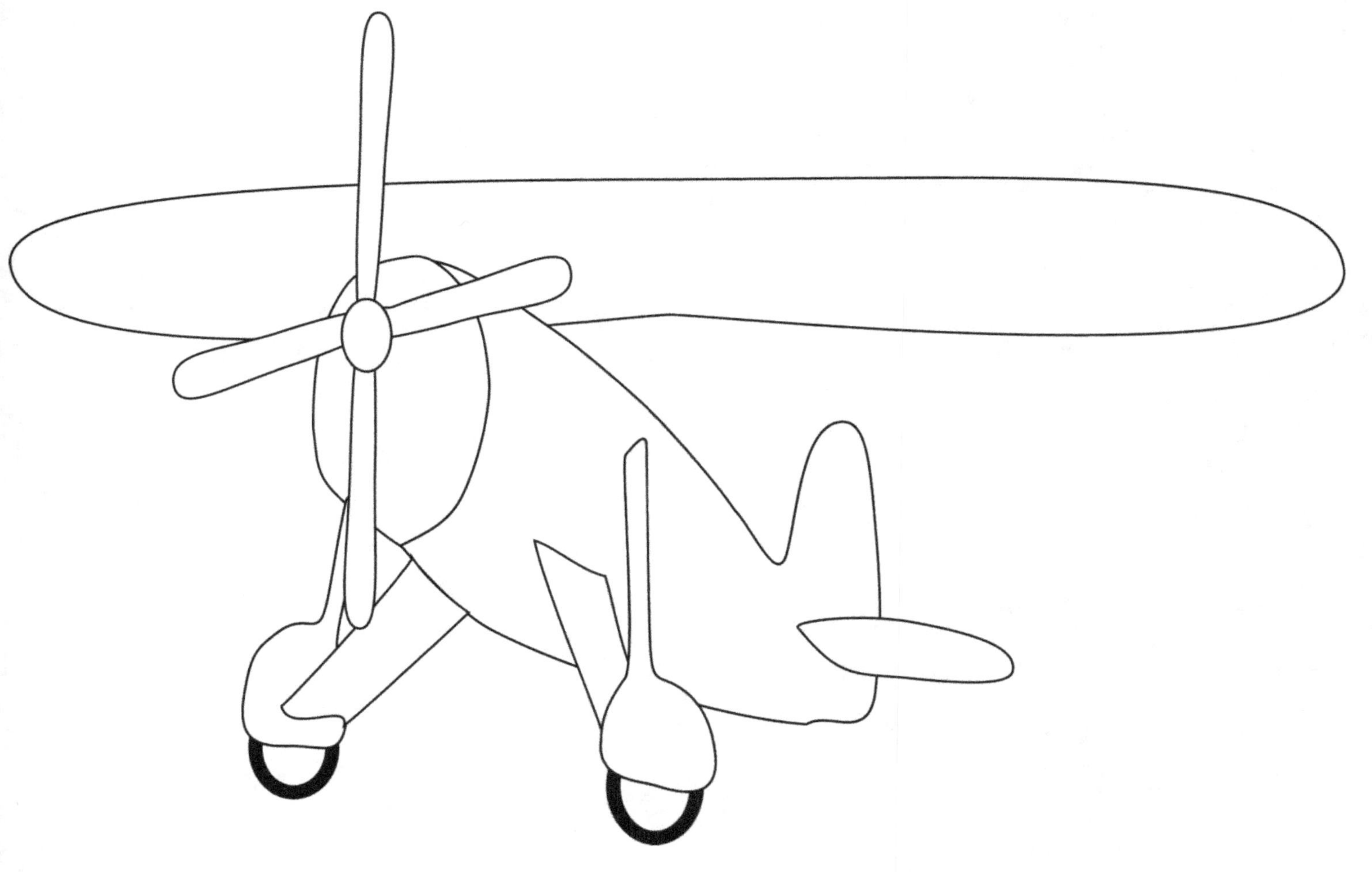

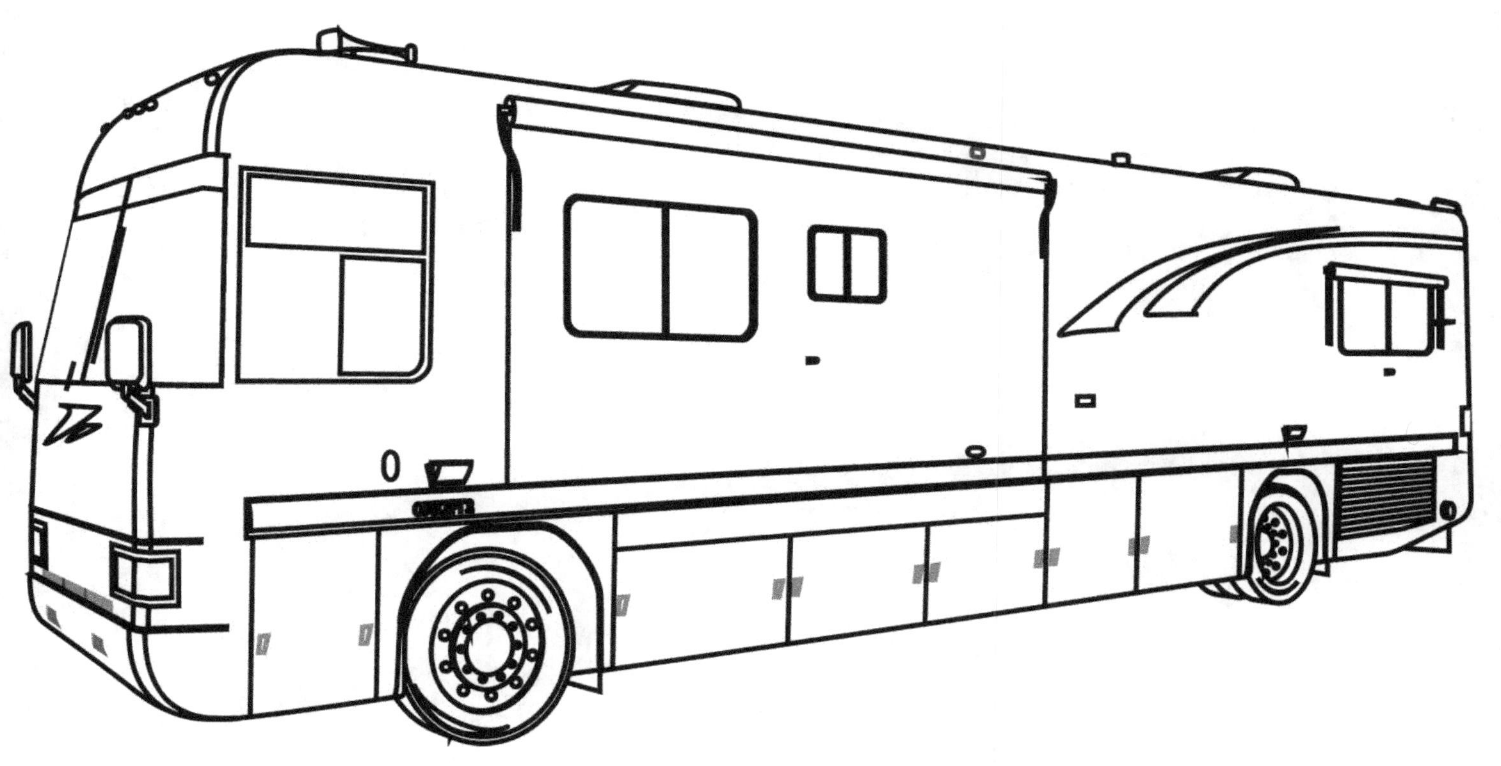

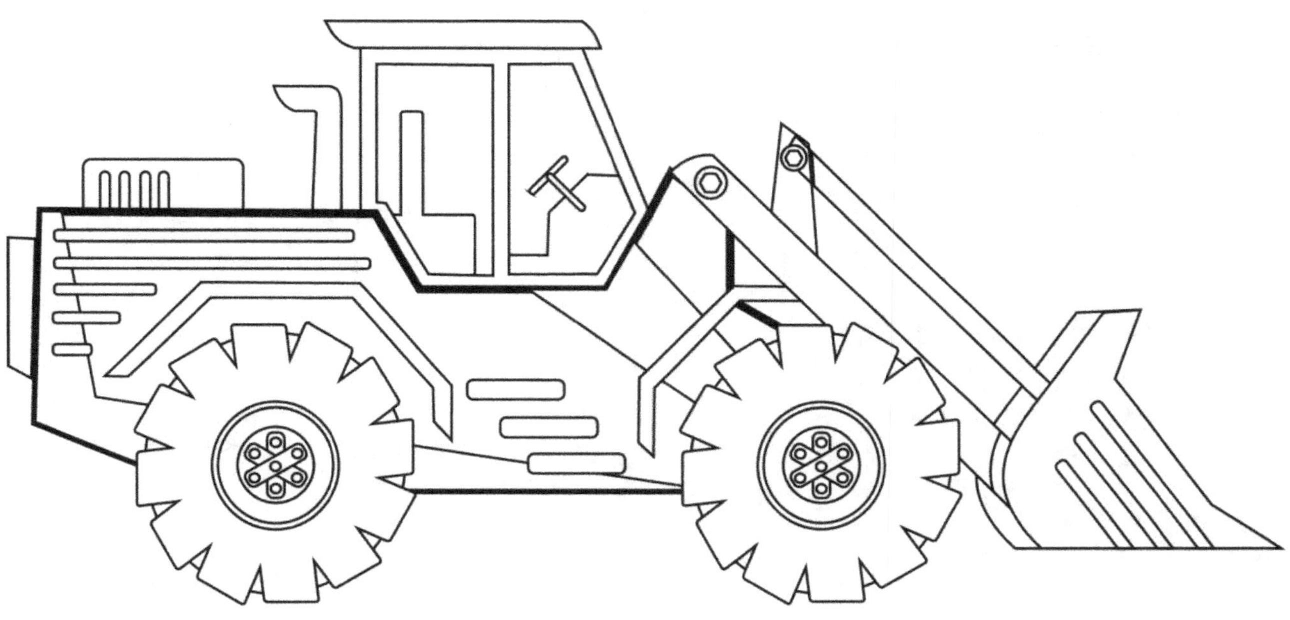

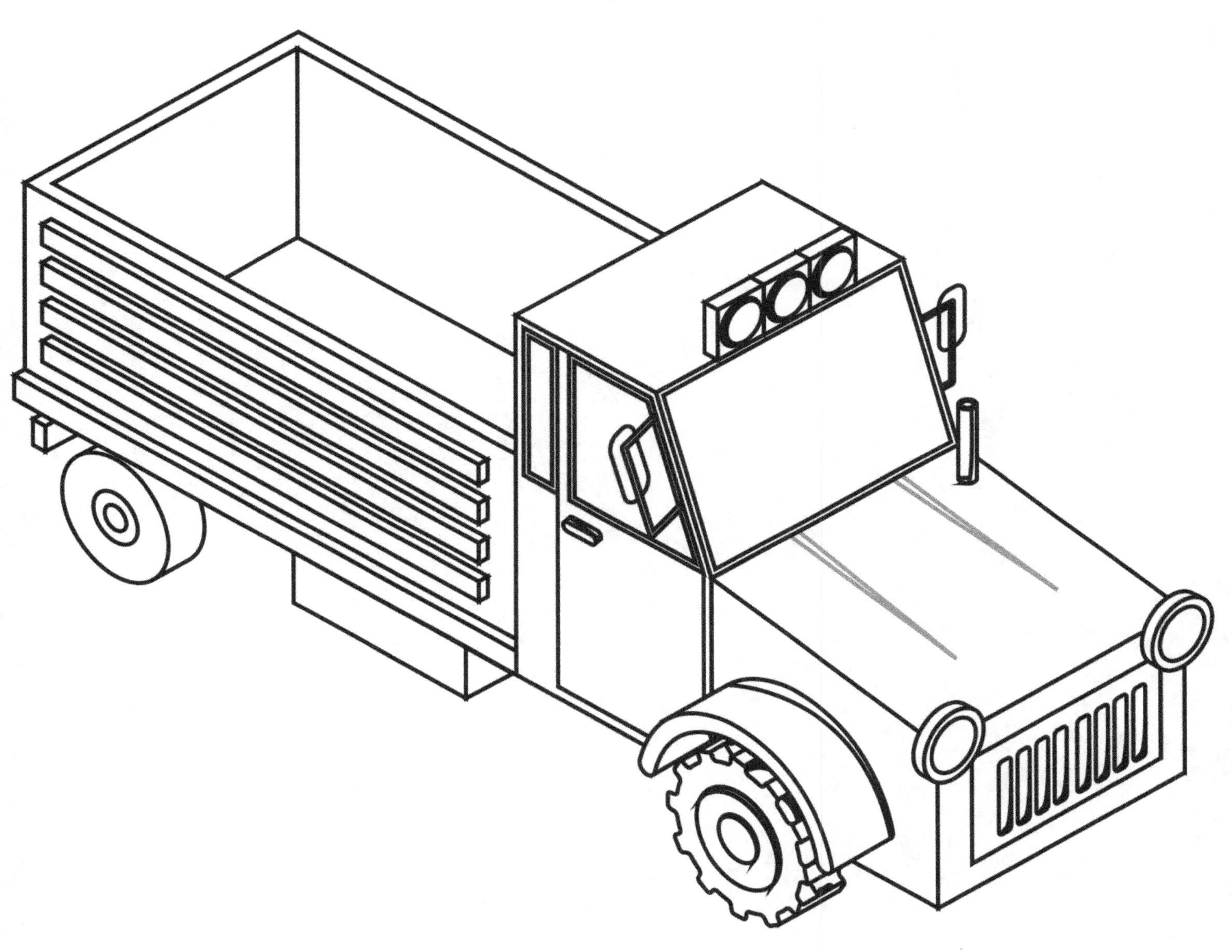

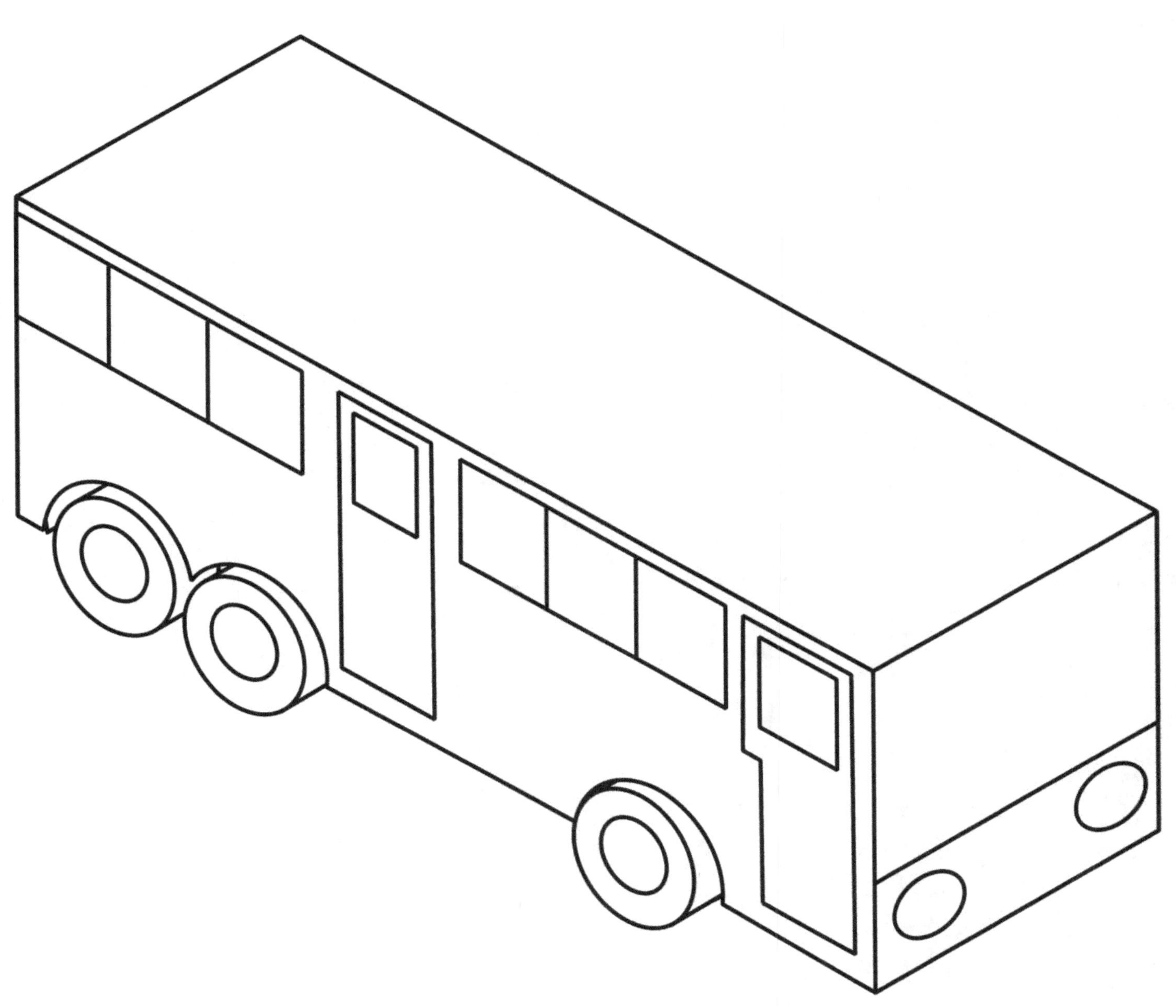

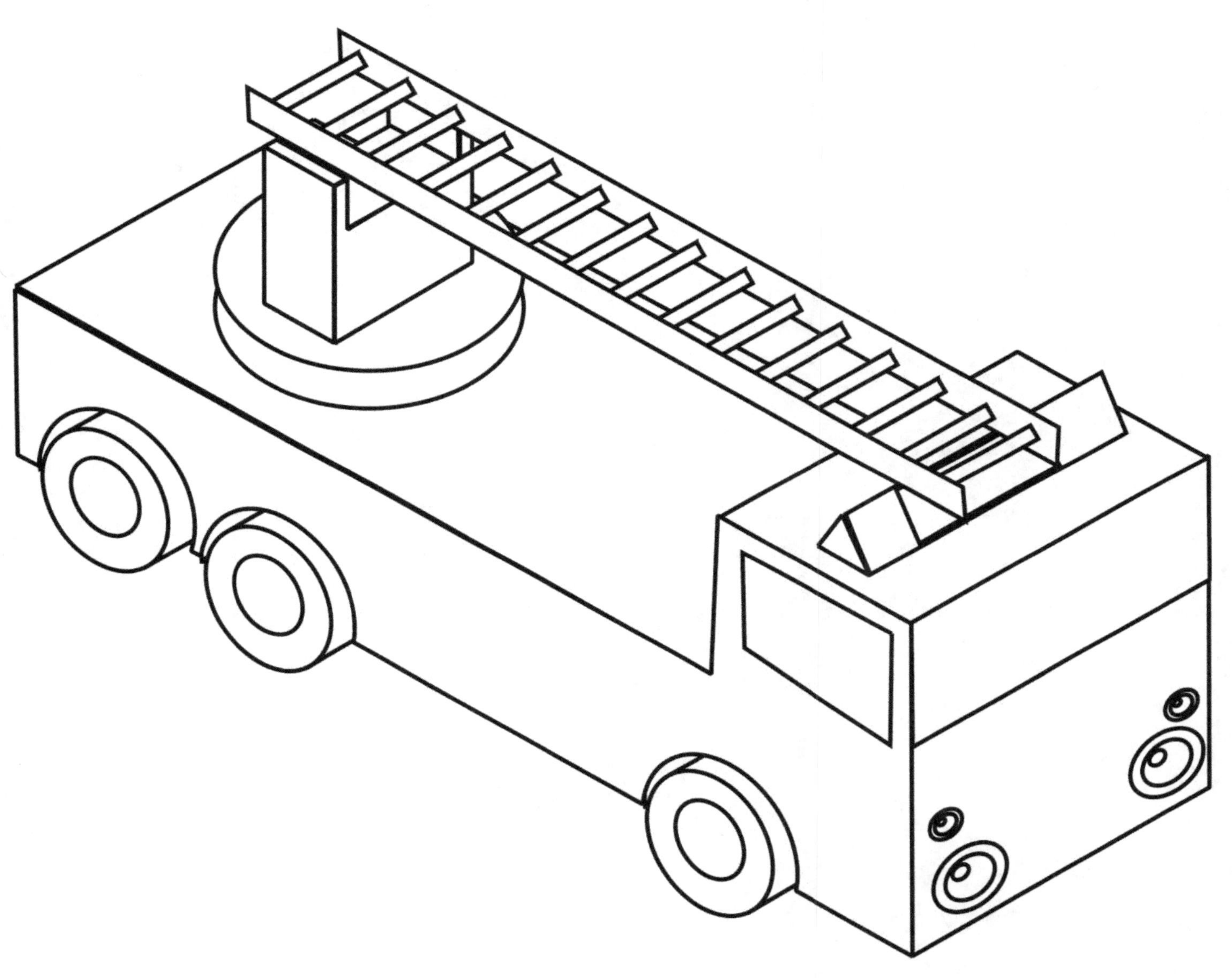

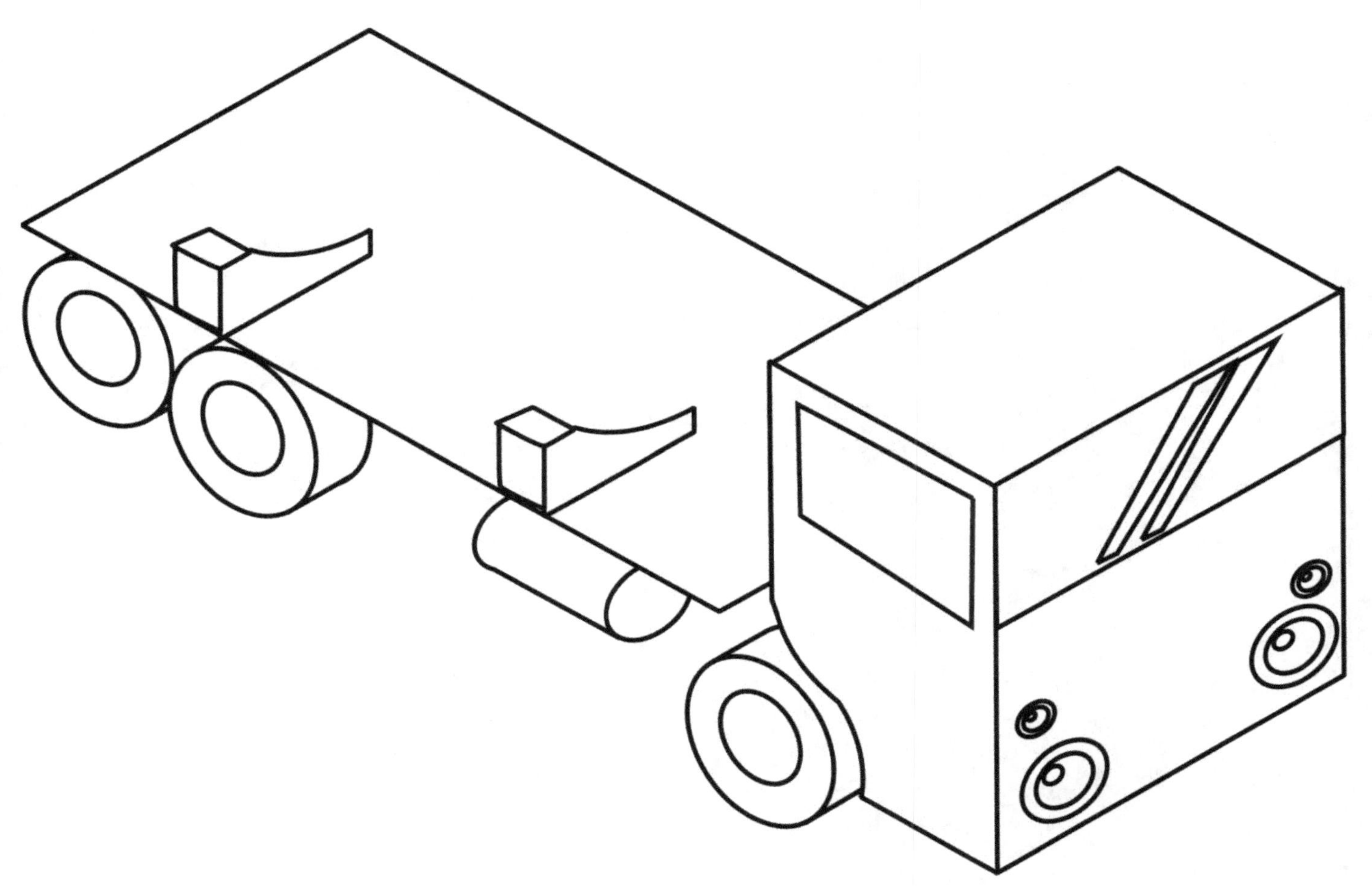